Pebble® Plus

The Dish on Mac and Cheese

by Catherine Ipcizade

Consulting Editor: Gail Saunders-Smith, PhD

Consultant: Professor Art Hill
Department of Food Science
University of Guelph

CAPSTONE PRESS
a capstone imprint

Pebble Plus is published by Capstone Press,
151 Good Counsel Drive, P.O. Box 669, Mankato, Minnesota 56002.
www.capstonepub.com

Books published by Capstone Press are manufactured with paper
containing at least 10 percent post-consumer waste.

Library of Congress Cataloging-in-Publication Data
Ipcizade, Catherine.
The dish on mac and cheese / by Catherine Ipcizade.
p. cm.—(Pebble plus. Favorite food facts)
Includes bibliographical references and index.
Summary: "Full-color photographs and simple text present fun facts about mac and cheese"—Provided by publisher.
ISBN 978-1-4296-6660-2 (library binding)
1. Cooking (Pasta)—Juvenile literature. I. Title. II. Series.
TX809.M17I63 2012
641.8'22—dc22   2011000370

Editorial Credits
Katy Kudela, editor; Heidi Thompson, designer; Svetlana Zhurkin, media researcher; Sarah Schuette, photo stylist;
Marcy Morin, scheduler; Laura Manthe, production specialist

Photo Credits
Capstone Studio/Karon Dubke, cover, 1, 4–5, 8–9, 10–11,
13, 15, 17, 18–19, 20–21, 21 (top right)
Mary Evans Picture Library, 7

Note to Parents and Teachers

The Favorite Food Facts series supports national social studies standards related to people,
places, and culture. This book describes and illustrates mac and cheese. The images support
early readers in understanding the text. The repetition of words and phrases helps early readers
learn new words. This book also introduces early readers to subject-specific vocabulary words,
which are defined in the Glossary section. Early readers may need assistance to read some
words and to use the Table of Contents, Glossary, Read More, Internet Sites, and Index sections
of the book.

Printed in the United States of America in North Mankato, Minnesota.
032011   006110CGF11

Table of Contents

A Cheesy Dish

People in the United States

eat lots of mac and cheese.

Stores sell more than

1 million boxes a day!

Inventing Mac and Cheese

Dried pasta came from China.

But the first mac and cheese recipe

came from Italy more than

700 years ago. People tossed

cooked noodles with Parmesan.

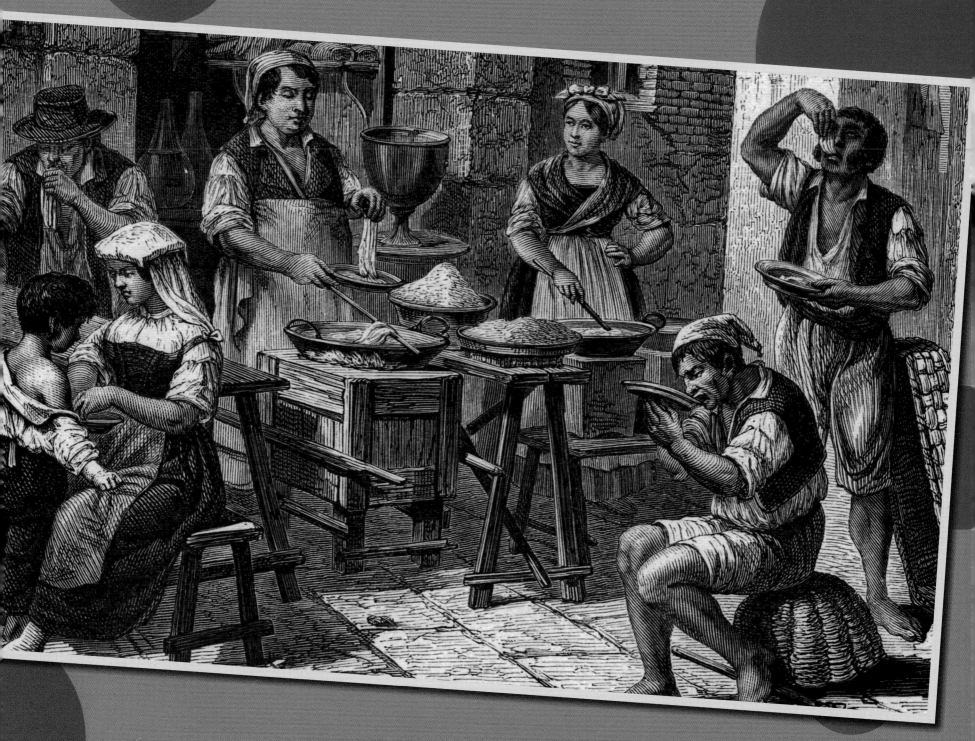

Since its start in 1937,

boxed mac and cheese

has been a top seller.

Stores sold the mix as "make

a meal for four in 9 minutes."

How It's Made

So many choices!

There are more than 600 kinds

of pasta. But most cooks pick

elbow macaroni to make

this cheesy dish.

Creamy cheese gives mac and cheese its color and flavor. Cheddar is the top cheese choice.

Imagine That!

Mac and cheese

is not just a dish.

It's also the color of a crayon!

This crayon is bright orange.

There are hundreds of
mac and cheese recipes.
Cooks mix in meat and
vegetables. They add fruit.
Some mix in chocolate!

It's served on a stick!

Fried mac and cheese

is a treat at state fairs.

People eat it plain.

They dip it in sauce.

More cheese, please.
Some people use mac and
cheese like a pizza crust.
How would you top your
mac and cheese pizza?

Make Pizza Mac

Here's a tasty way to use leftover mac and cheese. Be sure to ask an adult to help you use the oven.

Makes 4 to 6 servings

Here's what you need:

Ingredients	Equipment
2 cups (480 mL) leftover mac and cheese	bowl
	wooden spoon
2 eggs, slightly beaten	pie dish
½ cup (120 mL) pizza sauce	oven mitt
	pizza cutter
1 cup (240 mL) shredded cheese	
slices of tomato, and other toppings as you wish	

Here's what you do:

1. Preheat oven to 400 degrees Fahrenheit (200 degrees Celsius).
2. In a bowl, combine mac and cheese together with eggs. Mix well with a wooden spoon. Note: mac and cheese should be room temperature.
3. Pour mixture into pie dish and press down with a wooden spoon.
4. Bake dish in oven for 15 to 20 minutes, or until mac and cheese is slightly golden brown. Remove from oven.
5. Top mac and cheese "crust" with pizza sauce, shredded cheese, and tomatoes.
6. Bake pizza for 10 to 15 minutes, or until cheese melts.
7. Let pizza sit 10 minutes, then cut into slices and serve.

21

Glossary

cheddar—a hard yellow or white cheese

flavor—the kind of taste in a food

Parmesan—a hard dry sharply flavored cheese
that is sold grated or in wedges

pasta—a food made from flour and water,
then cut into shapes and dried

recipe—directions for making and cooking food

state fair—an outdoor show of farm products
and animals, often with entertainment, food,
games, and rides

Read More

Dolbear, Emily J. *How Did That Get to My Table? Pasta.* Community Connections. Ann Arbor, Mich.: Cherry Lake Pub., 2010.

Rotner, Shelley, and Gary Goss. *Where Does Food Come From?* Minneapolis: Millbrook Press, 2006.

Internet Sites

FactHound offers a safe, fun way to find Internet sites related to this book. All of the sites on FactHound have been researched by our staff.

Here's all you do:

Visit *www.facthound.com*

Type in this code: 9781429666602

Check out projects, games and lots more at
www.capstonekids.com

Index

Word Count: 198
Grade: 1
Early-Intervention Level: 20